CIGAR CURIOUS
101 Amusing Facts Rolled into One

Strange but Smoky: The Lighter Side of a Serious Craft

J.R. Johnson

THE AMERICAN CIGAR PRESS

2025

Cigar Curious: 101 Amusing Facts Rolled into One

© 2025 **J.R. Johnson**

All rights reserved. No part of this book may be reproduced, stored in a retrieval system, or transmitted in any form or by any means—electronic, mechanical, photocopying, recording, or otherwise—without prior written permission from the publisher, except for brief quotations in critical reviews or articles.

**Published by
The American Cigar Press**
A Publisher of History, Craft & Industry

ISBN: 979-8-9985117-2-1

For inquiries or permissions, visit:
www.TheAmericanCigarPress.com

Printed in the United States of America and other locations worldwide.

This book is a work of historical research. While every effort has been made to ensure accuracy, the author and publisher assume no responsibility for errors, omissions, or any consequences arising from its use.

Uncle Sam Approved.

Foreword

There's a peculiar joy in lighting a cigar—an act that demands patience in an age of speed, and silence in an age of noise. It's not just about smoke; it's about time, ritual, and the company of thought.

This book is a tribute to that experience. *Cigar Curious: 101 Amusing Facts Rolled into One* doesn't aim to chart the full history of cigars or prescribe the perfect cut. Instead, it invites you to wander—to pause at the edges of cigar lore, to enjoy the obscure, the unexpected, and the oddly delightful.

The entries appear in mostly random order, unbound by theme or chronology, to preserve an eclectic rhythm—more like a box of hand-rolled curiosities than a catalog. Each fact is grounded in careful research, with sources provided in the endnotes. The illustrations throughout are AI-generated: selected not for historical precision but to enhance the visual experience with a touch of imagination.

Whether you're an aficionado, a novice, or simply someone who appreciates the poetry of fire and leaf—welcome. May you find in these pages a few good companions for your next slow burn.

J.R. Johnson
June 2, 2028

Table of Contents

1. Where Does the Word "Cigar" Come From?
2. The Oldest Known Image of a Cigar Smoker
3. Seville: The Birthplace of the Modern Cigar
4. The First U.S. Cigar Factory
5. Tobacco Farming in the American Colonies
6. The Cuban Cigar Ban That Changed Everything
7. JFK's Secret Stash of Cuban Cigars
8. Mark Twain's Love Affair with Cigars
9. Ulysses S. Grant and His 10,000 Cigar Gift
10. Freud's Cigar Obsession—And His Most Famous Quote
11. Winston Churchill—A Cigar Icon
12. Fidel Castro and the Rise of Cohiba
13. The Origin of the Word "Stogie"
14. Civil War Soldiers Smoked & Traded Cigars on the Battlefield
15. The Lost Cigar Dispatch of 1862—Fact or Fiction?
16. Tampa—The Cigar Capital of the U.S.
17. America's Cigar Boom—8 Billion Smokes a Year
18. Napoleon's Surprising Cigar Preference
19. Mark Twain's Love for Cheap Cigars—And His Famous Prank
20. The 11-Hour Cigar Smoking Session—Fact or Fiction?
21. Cigars in World War II Rations
22. The Cuban Tradition of Women Cigar Rollers
23. Fidel Castro's Diplomatic Cigar Gifts
24. Cigar Box Tax Stamps—Tiny Artifacts of Tobacco History

25. Cigars as a Political Power Symbol
26. Cigars in Hollywood—A Symbol of Wealth & Power
27. George Burns' 100-Year Cigar Habit
28. Madonna & the Cigar Industry's Gender Shift
29. Bill Clinton, Cigars & a Political Scandal
30. Cuban Cigars—100% Handmade, No Machines Allowed
31. Ligero—The Powerhouse of a Cigar
32. The Year-Long Journey of a Premium Cigar
33. Cigars Aged for Decades—The Arturo Fuente "Añejo" Legacy
34. The 70/70 Rule—How to Keep Your Cigars Fresh
35. The World's Largest Cigar—A 295-Foot Masterpiece
36. Cigars Infused with Rum & Whiskey—A Flavorful Twist
37. Cigar-Smoking Geckos—Fact or Fiction?
38. The Longest Cigar Ash—A Fragile World Record?
39. Gurkha Cigars—The Brand Behind the World's Most Expensive Cigars
40. The Barber Pole Cigar—A Twisted Work of Art
41. The 12-Cigar Smoking World Record—Fact or Fiction?
42. "The Egg"—A Cigar Like No Other
43. Smoking Jackets—Fashion Born from the Cigar Ritual
44. The 600-Year-Old Cigar—An Ancient Find
45. Cigars—A Tradition of Celebration and Success
46. Al Capone & the Crime Boss Cigar Symbol
47. Writers & Their Cigar-Fueled Creativity
48. Tobacco in Native American Peace & Diplomacy
49. The First Flavored Cigars—A 1900s Innovation
50. Tobacco as a Sacred Offering in Native American Rituals

51. Early Tobacco Pipes—Artistic & Spiritual Masterpieces
52. The Return of Cigar Bars—Old-School Luxury Makes a Comeback
53. High-Tech Air Filtration in Modern Cigar Lounges
54. Cigars & Poker—A Gambler's Good Luck Charm?
55. Hand-Painted Cigar Bands—A Lost Art
56. The First International Cigar Competition—A Havana Mystery
57. Coffee-Infused Cigars—A Bold New Flavor Trend
58. Tobacco Giants & Their Private Farms
59. The Evolution of Tobacco Aging—Pressure-Aging Experiments
60. The First North American Tobacco Plantation—Jamestown, 1612
61. Tobacco Curing Barns—Colonial America's First Specialty Structures
62. The Tradition of "Toasting" a Cigar Before Lighting
63. The Wrapper—The Biggest Contributor to a Cigar's Flavor
64. The Invention of Cigar-Rolling Machines—A 19th Century Revolution
65. Cedar Spill Lighting—The Traditional Way to Fire Up
66. Cuban Cigar Testing—A Professional Smoker's Job
67. Cigar Bloom (Plume)—A Sign of Quality Aging
68. The "Razor-Sharp Burn Line"—A Sign of a Well-Made Cigar
69. Retrohaling—Unlocking Hidden Cigar Flavors
70. Bill Clinton's White House Cigar Celebration—Breaking the No-Smoking Rule
71. Fidel Castro's Poisoned Cigar Assassination Plot

72. Catholic Missionaries and the Global Spread of Tobacco Cultivation
73. Winston Churchill's Cigars Had Their Own Oxygen Mask
74. The FBI Used a Cigar Lounge to Bug a Mafia Boss
75. The First Cigar Smoker Was Imprisoned for Witchcraft
76. The Cigar Boom of the 1990s
77. The "Cigar of the Year" Effect
78. Tobacco Beetles—A Collector's Nightmare
79. The Difference Between Long-Filler and Short-Filler Cigars
80. The Role of Volado, Seco, and Ligero in a Blend
81. Cigar Tasting Wheels—Mapping Flavor Notes
82. Cigar Box Art—A Forgotten Americana Collectible
83. The Smoker's Cut vs. the Guillotine Cut
84. The Influence of Soil—Cigar Terroir
85. The "Fresh Roll" Cigars of Little Havana
86. Cigar Sommelier—A Real Job Title
87. Rolling Without a Mold—The *Entubado* Technique
88. The "Cold Draw" Ritual
89. The Art of Cigar Aging—Cedar's Secret Role
90. The Double Claro (Candela) Wrapper—A Green Revival
91. Celebrity-Owned Cigar Brands
92. The Secret Language of Cigar Bands
93. Women in the Modern Cigar Industry
94. The Cigar That Survived the Titanic
95. The First Cigar Vending Machine Was Coin-Operated in 1883
96. Cigar Ash in Paint? Artists Say Yes
97. Cigar-Toting Action Figures? G.I. Joe Once Had One

98. The Cigar Ring Gauge Tool Was Invented by a Watchmaker
99. The Only MLB No-Hitter Celebrated with a Cigar… on the Field
100. The Cigar-Shaped UFO—A Real Term in Ufology
101. The "Cigar Store Indian" Was Actually a Marketing Gimmick

101 Amusing Facts 1
List of Facts (By Category) 81
About the Author 87
Endnotes 88

101 Amusing Facts

1. Where Does the Word "Cigar" Come From?

The word *cigar* traces back to the Spanish *cigarro*, which itself likely originates from the Mayan word *sikar*, meaning "to smoke tobacco." Spanish explorers encountered tobacco use in the Americas and brought both the plant and the practice back to Europe in the 15th century. By the 18th and 19th centuries, cigars had become status symbols across European and American society. In English, the phonetic spelling "seegar" appeared frequently in early American writing, reflecting regional dialects and evolving trade vernacular. While "cigar" eventually standardized, "seegar" endures as a linguistic relic of tobacco's transatlantic journey.[1]

2. The Oldest Known Image of a Cigar Smoker

The earliest known depiction of cigar smoking appears on a 1,000-year-old Mayan pottery vessel, which shows a man inhaling from a rolled bundle of tobacco leaves. Discovered in Central America, the artifact offers striking evidence that the Mayans not only cultivated tobacco but also used it in ceremonial rituals and religious offerings. When Spanish explorers encountered these practices in the 15th century, they adopted and exported them—ushering in the global spread of cigar culture.[2]

3. Seville: The Birthplace of the Modern Cigar

The first commercial cigars were produced in Seville, Spain, in the early 1700s using Cuban-grown tobacco. Merchant ships carrying Virginia and Maryland tobacco to Europe began returning with expertly hand-rolled cigars from Seville—the city that perfected modern cigar-making in its Royal Tobacco Factory. These cigars, unlike traditional British smoking products, became highly desirable, influencing colonial American smoking habits.[3]

4. The First U.S. Cigar Factory

America's first recognized cigar factory was established in 1810 in Suffield, Connecticut, by Roswell and Samuel Viets. This pioneering venture marked the beginning of domestic cigar production in the United States. With tobacco farming expanding in the colonies, the demand for locally made cigars grew. Suffield, situated in the fertile Connecticut River Valley, became home to skilled rollers—many of them European immigrants—who helped launch a thriving industry that would later spread across the country.[4]

5. Tobacco Farming in the American Colonies

Virginia, Pennsylvania, and Maryland were among the first colonies to grow tobacco for cigars, each shaping the industry in unique ways. Virginia, the birthplace of American tobacco, produced naturally sweet, air-cured leaves. Maryland's Chesapeake region became known for its smooth, mild tobacco, well-suited for cigar wrappers. Pennsylvania, particularly Lancaster County, developed Pennsylvania Broadleaf, a dark, full-bodied variety ideal for strong cigar wrappers and filler. By the late 18th and early 19th centuries, these regions had firmly established themselves as leaders in American tobacco production.[5]

6. The Cuban Cigar Ban That Changed Everything

For decades, Cuban cigars dominated the U.S. market, prized for their quality and craftsmanship. That all changed in 1962, when the Cuban Embargo made importing them illegal. Practically overnight, American cigar lovers were forced to look elsewhere, leading to the rise of alternative cigar industries in the Dominican Republic, Nicaragua, and Honduras—countries that still produce many of today's top cigars.[6]

7. JFK's Secret Stash of Cuban Cigars

Before signing the Cuban Embargo, President John F. Kennedy made sure he wouldn't have to give up his favorite cigars. The night before issuing the ban, he secretly ordered 1,200 Cuban cigars, ensuring he had a personal supply before they became illegal. Only after confirming their delivery did he sign the embargo, effectively cutting off U.S. access to Cuban tobacco.[7]

8. Mark Twain's Love Affair with Cigars

Famed author Mark Twain was rarely seen without a cigar in hand, reportedly smoking 20 to 40 cigars a day. He once called cigars "his solace" and famously declared, "If I cannot smoke in heaven, then I shall not go." Though the exact number he smoked daily may be exaggerated, his love for cigars was undeniable, and they became an integral part of his public image.[8]

9. Ulysses S. Grant and His 10,000 Cigar Gift

After his 1862 victory at Fort Donelson, Union General Ulysses S. Grant was flooded with gifts—including an estimated 10,000 cigars. The surge followed newspaper reports showing him smoking during the battle, cementing his image as a cigar devotee. Grant later wrote, "In the account published in the papers I was represented as smoking a cigar in the midst of the conflict... As many as ten thousand were soon received." Though once a light smoker, he began consuming up to 20 cigars a day, a habit that endured for life. He eventually developed throat cancer, widely attributed to his heavy use.[9]

10. Freud's Cigar Obsession—And His Most Famous Quote

Sigmund Freud reportedly smoked 20 cigars a day, believing they enhanced his concentration and self-control. He once remarked to his doctor, "I believe I owe to the cigar a great intensification of my capacity to work and a facilitation of my self control." Despite being diagnosed with oral cancer in 1923, Freud continued smoking until his death in 1939. The phrase "Sometimes a cigar is just a cigar" is widely attributed to Freud, suggesting that not every object holds symbolic meaning. However, there is no evidence he ever said or wrote this, and it contradicts his theory that even trivial actions have significance.[10]

11. Winston Churchill—A Cigar Icon

British Prime Minister Winston Churchill was rarely seen without a cigar, and his iconic image—cane in hand, cigar clenched in teeth—became a symbol of wartime defiance and personal resolve. He favored Cuban brands like Romeo y Julieta and La Aroma de Cuba, often smoking eight to ten cigars a day. His preference for large, robust cigars led to the naming of the "Churchill" size in his honor: a long, thick vitola that remains popular among aficionados today.[11]

12. Fidel Castro and the Rise of Cohiba

Fidel Castro's affinity for cigars led to the creation of the Cohiba brand in the 1960s, initially produced exclusively for Cuban government officials and diplomats. These premium cigars were not available to the public, enhancing their allure and making them one of the most sought-after Cuban smokes in history. In 1982, coinciding with the FIFA World Cup in Spain, Cohibas were officially released for public sale, marking the first time regular consumers could purchase them.[12]

13. The Origin of the Word "Stogie"

The term "stogie" traces back to Conestoga, Pennsylvania, where long, thin cigars were made for wagon drivers in the 1800s. These cigars were cheap, durable, and easy to smoke while traveling, making them a staple among early American pioneers.[13]

14. Civil War Soldiers Smoked & Traded Cigars on the Battlefield

Cigars were a common sight during the Civil War, with soldiers from both the Union and Confederacy turning to tobacco as a small comfort amid hardship. Carried in knapsacks and coat pockets, cigars served as both personal solace and informal currency. Between battles, opposing soldiers sometimes exchanged cigars across lines, using them as spontaneous peace offerings during moments of ceasefire or shared encampment. These exchanges offered rare glimpses of humanity amid the brutality of war—proof that even under fire, a good smoke could bring men together.[14]

15. The Lost Cigar Dispatch of 1862—Fact or Fiction?

One of the most famous cigar-related war stories comes from the Civil War, when a Union soldier allegedly found a Confederate battle plan wrapped around three cigars near Frederick, Maryland. The documents, known as Special Order 191, revealed General Robert E. Lee's movements and allowed Union forces to intercept the Confederate army at the Battle of Antietam—one of the war's most decisive clashes. While the discovery of the orders is a verified historical event, the idea that they were wrapped around cigars remains debated, with limited primary sources confirming that detail.[15]

16. Tampa—The Cigar Capital of the U.S.

By the 1920s, Tampa, Florida, had earned the nickname "Cigar City," with Ybor City at its heart. Founded in 1886 by Vicente Martinez Ybor, the district became a hub for Cuban, Spanish, and Eastern European immigrants who hand-rolled premium cigars. At its peak, Tampa housed approximately 200 cigar factories employing around 10,000 workers, producing nearly 500 million cigars annually.[16]

17. America's Cigar Boom—8 Billion Smokes a Year

In 1920, the United States reached its zenith in cigar production, turning out more than 8 billion cigars in a single year. This golden era was fueled by rising consumer demand, the growing popularity of tobacco across class lines, and a major technological leap: the invention of automated short-filler cigar machines. These machines revolutionized production, allowing factories to roll cigars at unprecedented speed and scale. While hand-rolled cigars remained a premium product, mass production made cigars accessible to nearly every corner of American society.[17]

18. Napoleon's Surprising Cigar Preference

Napoleon Bonaparte was known for his prodigious use of snuff, a powdered tobacco inhaled through the nose, rather than for smoking cigars. He maintained an extensive collection of snuffboxes and was rarely seen without one. While Spain had a significant tobacco trade and produced cigars in cities like Seville and Cádiz, there is no credible evidence to suggest that Napoleon favored Spanish cigars over Cuban ones. In fact, Cuban cigars did not gain widespread popularity in Europe until after Napoleon's era.[18]

19. Mark Twain's Love for Cheap Cigars—And His Famous Prank

Mark Twain was renowned for his fondness for inexpensive cigars, often choosing rough domestic brands over fancier imports. Despite being one of the most celebrated literary figures of his time, Twain had little patience for pretension—especially when it came to tobacco. He once quipped, "I know a good cigar better than you do, for I know a bad cigar better than anybody else. I judge by the price only; if it costs above 5 cents, I know it is a bad cigar."

An illustrative anecdote recounts how Twain, upon being offered expensive imported cigars by a friend, politely declined and asked for his usual cheap ones instead. The friend, hoping to disprove Twain's theory, later swapped in high-end cigars under the guise of his usual brand. Twain lit up, puffed a few times, and complained they tasted worse than usual. The incident, whether apocryphal or not, served as a witty reminder of Twain's deeply held belief that luxury was often just an illusion—and price a poor indicator of pleasure.

Twain's consistent preference for budget cigars wasn't just a matter of taste. It reflected his broader skepticism toward societal pretensions and the commodification of refinement. For him, cigars were for thinking, not showing off—and the less expensive, the better.[19]

20. The 11-Hour Cigar Smoking Session—Fact or Fiction?

A persistent legend in cigar circles claims that someone once smoked a single cigar continuously for over 11 hours without relighting. While slow-burning cigars and extended smoking sessions are celebrated among aficionados, such an uninterrupted duration seems implausible given the natural burn rate of even the largest cigars. The longest verified durations in official competitions, such as the Cigar Smoking World Championship, typically range between 3 to 4 hours. No credible documentation supports the 11-hour claim, suggesting it is more likely an urban legend or exaggerated anecdote.[20]

21. Cigars in World War II Rations

During World War II, the U.S. military included tobacco products in soldiers' rations to boost morale. Cigarettes were commonly distributed to enlisted men, often included in K-rations. While cigars were less prevalent, they were occasionally provided, particularly to officers and higher-ranking personnel, reflecting their status as symbols of leadership and prestige. Veteran testimonies and historical records indicate that cigars, though not standard issue, were among the small luxuries that offered comfort amidst the hardships of war.[21]

22. The Cuban Tradition of Women Cigar Rollers

In Cuba, women known as *torcedoras* have become an iconic part of the cigar industry. Though cigar rolling was long dominated by men, the post-revolutionary period saw the rise of highly skilled female rollers, particularly at the famed El Laguito factory—home of the Cohiba brand. Women were believed to have the dexterity and patience ideal for rolling elegant, complex vitolas.

One of the most respected figures was María Sierra, among the first female master rollers, whose precision helped elevate the status of *torcedoras*. Today, women continue to produce some of Cuba's most sought-after cigars, blending craft, tradition, and cultural pride.[22]

23. Fidel Castro's Diplomatic Cigar Gifts

Fidel Castro masterfully wielded cigars not merely as personal indulgences but as instruments of diplomacy. Throughout his rule, he gifted Cuban cigars—most notably Cohibas—to world leaders, diplomats, and influential allies. These cigars, initially reserved for high-ranking officials and foreign dignitaries, became emblems of Cuban prestige and craftsmanship. In gifting them, Castro reinforced Cuba's image as the global epicenter of premium tobacco, while subtly cultivating goodwill and influence. Over time, many of these cigars became rare collectibles, further adding to the mystique of Cuba's cigar legacy and the political theater surrounding them.[23]

24. Cigar Box Tax Stamps—Tiny Artifacts of Tobacco History

In the late 19th and early 20th centuries, U.S. cigar boxes were sealed with ornate tax stamps, issued by the federal government to verify payment of excise duties. These stamps, often detailed with fine engraving and patriotic imagery, were both regulatory tools and miniature works of art. Collectors now prize these fragile slips of paper, which not only authenticated the cigars inside but also captured a vivid slice of economic and design history. Changes in stamp colors and formats can help date boxes precisely, making them valuable clues for cigar historians and memorabilia enthusiasts.[24]

25. Cigars as a Political Power Symbol

Smoking a cigar was once seen as a political statement, particularly among world leaders. Figures like Winston Churchill, Fidel Castro, and Theodore Roosevelt famously used cigars as part of their public image, reinforcing their authority and presence. In diplomatic settings, cigars were often exchanged as symbols of power and negotiation, with leaders using them to project confidence and influence. Even today, cigars remain a status symbol, though their overt political significance has faded over time.[25]

26. Cigars in Hollywood—A Symbol of Wealth & Power

In Hollywood cinema, cigars have long served as a visual shorthand for power, wealth, and dominance. Characters such as Gordon Gekko in *Wall Street* (1987), Tony Montana in *Scarface* (1983), and Don Vito Corleone in *The Godfather* (1972) are often depicted with cigars, reinforcing their status and authority. This cinematic trope underscores the cultural perception of cigars as luxuries reserved for the elite.[26]

27. George Burns' 100-Year Cigar Habit

Legendary comedian George Burns was rarely seen without a cigar and famously smoked them until the age of 100. He often credited cigars for his longevity and sense of humor, joking, "If I'd taken my doctor's advice and quit smoking when he advised me to, I wouldn't have lived to go to his funeral." Though his claim that cigars contributed to his long life is anecdotal, Burns remains one of Hollywood's most iconic cigar smokers.[27]

28. Madonna & the Cigar Industry's Gender Shift

In the 1990s, Madonna made headlines by publicly smoking cigars, challenging the long-held notion that cigars were strictly a man's luxury. Her appearances with cigars in interviews, photo shoots, and music videos helped shift the industry's marketing approach, opening the door for women cigar smokers. Today, more women than ever enjoy premium cigars, thanks in part to cultural figures like Madonna reshaping the image of cigar smoking.[28]

29. Bill Clinton, Cigars & a Political Scandal

President Bill Clinton was a known cigar aficionado, but in the 1990s, cigars took on a far more controversial role in American political history. During the investigation into the Monica Lewinsky affair, it was revealed that a cigar had been used in one of the most infamous episodes of the scandal—transforming an otherwise refined indulgence into a symbol of political spectacle. The incident left an indelible mark on the cultural memory of cigars, intertwining them with tabloid headlines and late-night monologues. Despite the fallout, Clinton's enjoyment of cigars remained well-documented, with some reports suggesting a preference for high-end brands like Gurkha.[29]

30. Cuban Cigars—100% Handmade, No Machines Allowed

One defining feature of Cuban cigars is that they are made entirely by hand, with no machines involved in the rolling process. Skilled *torcedores* (cigar rollers) meticulously sort, bunch, and roll each cigar using traditional techniques passed down for generations. Unlike mass-produced cigars, Cuban cigars rely on human craftsmanship to ensure quality, consistency, and an exceptional smoking experience.[30]

31. Ligero—The Powerhouse of a Cigar

The ligero leaf is the strongest and most flavorful part of a cigar, found at the top of the tobacco plant, where it receives the most sunlight. These leaves are thicker, darker, and packed with intense nicotine and spice, making them essential for full-bodied cigar blends. Master blenders use ligero carefully, balancing its boldness with milder leaves to create complexity and depth in premium cigars.[31]

32. The Year-Long Journey of a Premium Cigar

A high-quality, hand-rolled cigar can take up to a year or more to produce, from planting the tobacco seed to final aging. After months of careful cultivation, the leaves undergo fermentation, drying, and meticulous rolling, followed by extended aging to refine flavors. Some ultra-premium cigars even age for several years before reaching the market, ensuring the perfect balance of aroma, burn, and taste.[32]

33. Cigars Aged for Decades—The Arturo Fuente "Añejo" Legacy

Some cigars are aged for decades before being released, allowing the tobacco to develop extraordinary smoothness and complexity. One famous example is Arturo Fuente's "Añejo" line, which uses tobacco aged in cognac barrels for years, creating a rich, refined profile. Other brands, like Davidoff and Padrón, also release limited-aged cigars, with some rare editions resting for 20+ years before hitting the shelves.[33]

34. The 70/70 Rule—How to Keep Your Cigars Fresh

The gold standard for cigar storage is the "70/70 Rule": 70 degrees Fahrenheit and 70% relative humidity. This balance preserves a cigar's essential oils, prevents cracking or mold, and ensures an even burn with optimal flavor. Deviating too far in either direction—too dry or too moist—can compromise the draw, aroma, and structure. A quality humidor, equipped with a reliable hygrometer and humidification system, helps maintain these ideal conditions. When properly stored, premium cigars can remain in peak condition for years, aging like fine wine.[34]

35. The World's Largest Cigar—A 295-Foot Masterpiece

In August 2016, Cuban master cigar roller José Castelar Cairo, known as "Cueto," crafted the world's longest hand-rolled cigar, measuring an astounding 90 meters (295 feet). This monumental creation was dedicated to Fidel Castro's 90th birthday and was assembled over ten days with the assistance of several helpers. The cigar, made using approximately 80 kilograms of tobacco, was displayed in Havana's Morro-Cabaña fortress, symbolizing Cuba's rich cigar heritage and craftsmanship.[35]

36. Cigars Infused with Rum & Whiskey—A Flavorful Twist

Some cigars are infused with rum, whiskey, cognac, or even coffee to enhance their flavor profile. Brands like Arturo Fuente's "Añejo" line feature Connecticut Broadleaf wrappers aged in cognac barrels, imparting a rich and unique taste. Similarly, Drew Estate's "ACID" cigars are known for their infusion process, where tobaccos are cured in aroma rooms with a blend of essential oils, herbs, and botanicals, creating distinctive aromatic profiles. While traditionalists may prefer classic cigars, these infused varieties offer a flavorful alternative that has gained popularity among modern smokers.[36]

37. Cigar-Smoking Geckos—Fact or Fiction?

One of the more peculiar cigar myths claims that geckos in cigar factories "smoke" cigars—either by crawling into smoldering leaves or basking near lit cigars. While small lizards are occasionally found in warm, humid warehouses, there's no scientific evidence that they seek out smoke or tobacco. The story is best understood as a blend of urban legend, visual coincidence, and cigar lounge humor—but it's a colorful tale all the same.[37]

38. The Longest Cigar Ash—A Fragile World Record?

The longest cigar ash ever recorded is said to have stretched over 7 inches without breaking. While many cigar smokers take pride in keeping their ash intact, no official Guinness World Record confirms this feat. "Long ash" contests are common in lounges and among hobbyists, but claims beyond a few inches remain unverified—and likely exaggerated.[38]

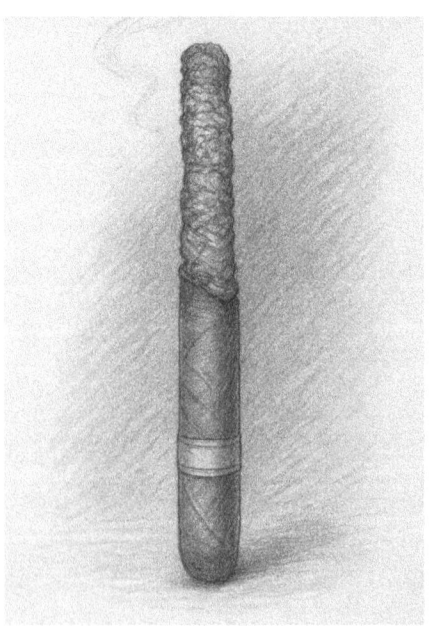

39. Gurkha Cigars—The Brand Behind the World's Most Expensive Cigars

Gurkha Cigars is a luxury cigar brand renowned for producing some of the world's most exclusive and expensive cigars. Founded in 1989 by Kaizad Hansotia, the company transformed from a small, obscure brand into a high-end boutique cigar line catering to collectors and affluent smokers. The brand name "Gurkha" is inspired by the legendary Gurkha warriors of Nepal, known for their fierce loyalty and strength, which the company uses to symbolize craftsmanship and prestige. Gurkha is famous for ultra-premium cigars, including the Gurkha Royal Courtesan ($1.36 million per cigar) and His Majesty's Reserve ($75,000 per box), both infused with rare cognacs. Their cigars often use aged Dominican and Nicaraguan tobaccos, and many are presented in ornate packaging, making them highly sought after by collectors. While some cigar purists argue that Gurkha cigars are overpriced and overhyped, they remain a status symbol in the cigar world, associated with luxury, exclusivity, and indulgence.[39]

40. The Barber Pole Cigar—A Twisted Work of Art

Barber Pole cigars stand out with their striped design, created by twisting two contrasting wrapper leaves—typically a light Connecticut Shade and a dark Maduro—around the cigar. The result is more than visual flair: each puff blends the creamy notes of the lighter leaf with the bold richness of the darker one. Though sometimes seen as novelty smokes, they require real craftsmanship and offer a complex, shifting flavor experience.[40]

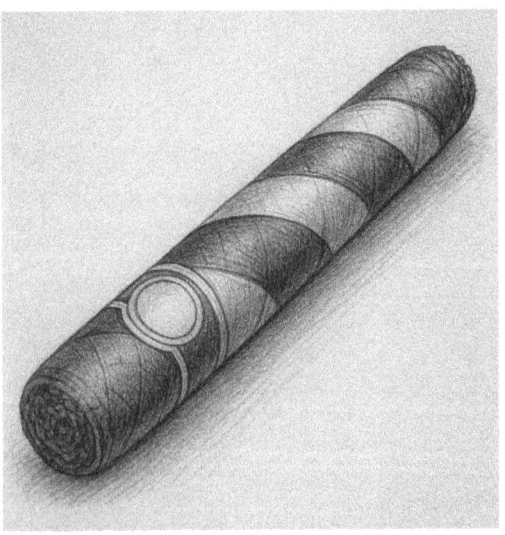

41. The 12-Cigar Smoking World Record—Fact or Fiction?

A persistent claim suggests someone once smoked 12 cigars at the same time, setting an unofficial world record. But no credible documentation confirms it. Lighting, drawing, and maintaining that many cigars simultaneously poses obvious challenges, making this tale more cigar lounge folklore than fact.[41]

42. "The Egg"—A Cigar Like No Other

One of the strangest cigars ever produced, "The Egg" defies all expectations of traditional cigar design. Created by Drew Estate, this novelty cigar features a bulbous, egg-shaped midsection that swells dramatically from its tapered ends—resembling a cigar with a hard-boiled surprise at its center. The unusual shape makes it notoriously difficult to roll and even more challenging to smoke evenly. Still, "The Egg" remains a cult favorite among collectors and aficionados drawn to its sheer oddity. It's not about balance or burn—it's about bragging rights and the love of the unexpected.[42]

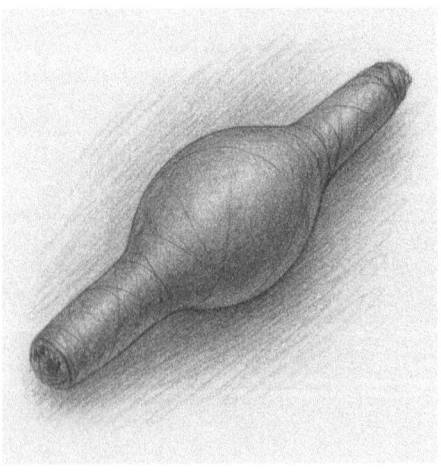

43. Smoking Jackets—Fashion Born from the Cigar Ritual

The smoking jacket emerged in the 19th century as a stylish way to protect evening clothes from smoke, ash, and odor. Made of velvet or silk, it became a symbol of leisure and refinement among gentlemen. Though no longer everyday wear, it still appears in luxury fashion and upscale cigar lounges as a nostalgic nod to old-world elegance.[43]

44. The 600-Year-Old Cigar—An Ancient Find

The oldest known cigar was discovered in a tomb in Guatemala, estimated to be over 600 years old. Archaeologists believe the cigar, found among other ceremonial artifacts, was rolled by the Mayan civilization, which is credited with being one of the earliest cultures to enjoy tobacco. While the find provides fascinating insight into ancient smoking traditions, documentation is scarce, and the exact origins remain debated among historians.[44]

45. Cigars—A Tradition of Celebration and Success

Throughout history, cigars have been a symbol of celebration, commonly enjoyed at weddings, business deals, and major life milestones. Lighting a cigar has long been associated with marking achievements, from the birth of a child to sealing an important contract. This tradition spans multiple cultures, where cigars represent luxury, success, and camaraderie. Even today, the ritual of sharing a fine cigar remains a cherished way to commemorate special occasions.[45]

46. Al Capone & the Crime Boss Cigar Symbol

Famous crime bosses like Al Capone were rarely seen without a cigar in hand, using it as a symbol of power, wealth, and intimidation. During the Prohibition era, cigars became a staple among gangsters, reinforcing their high-status image while running lucrative bootlegging empires. Capone, along with other mob bosses, used cigars to project a sense of control, sophistication, and dominance—an image still associated with the underworld in pop culture today.[46]

47. Writers & Their Cigar-Fueled Creativity

Famous literary figures like Ernest Hemingway and Rudyard Kipling were devoted cigar smokers, often lighting up while writing. Hemingway, known for his rugged lifestyle and love for Cuban cigars, found inspiration in the smoke-filled air of Havana's bars. Kipling, author of *The Jungle Book*, even referenced cigars in his famous poem "The Betrothed", declaring, "A woman is only a woman, but a good cigar is a smoke." Both writers saw cigars as an essential part of their creative process, making them a staple in the literary world.[47]

48. Tobacco in Native American Peace & Diplomacy

For centuries, Native American tribes used tobacco in peace negotiations and diplomatic ceremonies, offering it as a symbol of trust, respect, and unity. Smoking a peace pipe, often filled with sacred tobacco, was a ritual practiced by many tribes to seal agreements and forge alliances. These ceremonies played a crucial role in conflict resolution, trade negotiations, and tribal diplomacy, reinforcing tobacco's deep cultural significance beyond personal use.[48]

49. The First Flavored Cigars—A 1900s Innovation

Flavored cigars date back to the early 1900s, when manufacturers began experimenting with infusing tobacco with rum, vanilla, and other flavors. Early blends aimed to enhance the natural sweetness of the tobacco, appealing to smokers who preferred a smoother, more aromatic experience. Over time, this practice evolved into the modern infused cigar industry, with brands like Acid, Tatiana, and Java by Drew Estate continuing the tradition of uniquely flavored cigars.[49]

50. Tobacco as a Sacred Offering in Native American Rituals

Many Native American tribes considered tobacco a sacred plant, using it as an offering to the spirits in religious rituals. Tobacco was often sprinkled onto fires, placed in sacred locations, or smoked in ceremonial pipes as a way to communicate with ancestors, seek guidance, or express gratitude. This practice, still observed in some Indigenous communities today, highlights tobacco's spiritual and cultural significance beyond its recreational use.[50]

51. Early Tobacco Pipes—Artistic & Spiritual Masterpieces

Before cigars became widespread, early tobacco pipes were often intricate works of art, reflecting deep cultural and spiritual significance. Many Native American tribes crafted pipes from stone, clay, and wood, often carving them into animal shapes, human figures, or sacred symbols. These pipes were not just smoking tools but spiritual artifacts, used in ceremonies, rituals, and storytelling traditions. Today, many of these early pipes are preserved in museums as testaments to the artistry and heritage of Indigenous cultures.[51]

52. The Return of Cigar Bars—Old-School Luxury Makes a Comeback

The resurgence of cigar bars in major cities is part of a larger trend toward "old-school luxury", where vintage-style experiences like cocktail lounges, bespoke tailoring, and fine cigars are making a comeback. Upscale cigar lounges in cities like New York, London, and Miami cater to a new generation of cigar enthusiasts seeking a refined, social atmosphere. This revival reflects a broader cultural shift toward craftsmanship, heritage, and indulgence in classic luxuries.[52]

53. High-Tech Air Filtration in Modern Cigar Lounges

Unlike the smoky, dimly lit cigar lounges of the past, today's high-end cigar bars feature advanced air filtration systems to create a comfortable, smoke-friendly environment. These systems use HEPA filters, air exchange technology, and charcoal filtration to clear the air, allowing guests to enjoy cigars without overwhelming smoke buildup. Many luxury cigar lounges invest heavily in ventilation technology, making them more welcoming to both seasoned aficionados and newcomers.[53]

54. Cigars & Poker—A Gambler's Good Luck Charm?

Some professional poker players swear that smoking a cigar helps them stay focused and maintain a calm demeanor at the table. The slow-burning nature of a cigar allows players to pace themselves, control their nerves, and project confidence, creating an edge in high-stakes games. While there's no scientific proof that cigars improve poker performance, the image of a cigar-smoking card shark remains a classic symbol in gambling culture and casino lore.[54]

55. Hand-Painted Cigar Bands—A Lost Art

Before mass printing technology was developed, cigar bands were hand-painted, often featuring intricate designs and gold accents. These bands were used to brand cigars, distinguish premium products, and appeal to wealthy smokers. While mass production eventually replaced hand-painted bands, some high-end cigar manufacturers still use embossed foil and detailed printing techniques to maintain the elegance of classic cigar branding.[55]

56. The First International Cigar Competition—A Havana Mystery

A widely circulated claim states that the first-ever international cigar competition was held in Havana in 1935, bringing together master cigar rollers from across the world. However, historical records on this event are scarce, making it difficult to verify whether it was an official competition or a private industry gathering. While Havana has long been the center of the cigar world, more research is needed to confirm this fascinating but elusive piece of cigar history.[56]

57. Coffee-Infused Cigars—A Bold New Flavor Trend

Some cigar manufacturers are experimenting with non-traditional ingredients like coffee-infused tobacco, creating a richer, more aromatic smoking experience. Brands like Drew Estate's Tabak Especial and Java by Rocky Patel have pioneered this approach, blending premium tobaccos with coffee flavors to enhance the smoking experience. This modern twist on cigar-making appeals to both traditional smokers and those seeking unique, flavored cigars.[57]

58. Tobacco Giants & Their Private Farms

The largest cigar manufacturers own and operate their own tobacco farms, ensuring complete quality control from seed to cigar. Companies like Arturo Fuente, Davidoff, and Oliva grow tobacco on carefully selected land in the Dominican Republic, Nicaragua, and Cuba, refining every aspect of the cultivation process. By controlling their own farms, these companies can maintain consistency, experiment with aging techniques, and produce some of the world's most sought-after cigars.[58]

59. The Evolution of Tobacco Aging—Pressure-Aging Experiments

Tobacco aging techniques are evolving, with some manufacturers experimenting with pressure-aging methods to accelerate the process while preserving rich flavors. This involves exposing tobacco leaves to controlled pressure, humidity, and temperature to replicate the natural aging process more efficiently. While traditionalists argue that slow aging produces the best cigars, some modern brands are embracing innovation to create new smoking experiences.[59]

60. The First North American Tobacco Plantation—Jamestown, 1612

John Rolfe's 1612 introduction of *Nicotiana tabacum*—a sweeter Caribbean strain of tobacco—into Jamestown, Virginia, marked a foundational moment in American agriculture. This innovation not only rescued the struggling colony's economy but also laid the groundwork for tobacco to become Virginia's primary export by 1624. Rolfe's success established key economic patterns—standardization, specialization, and market-driven production—that would define early American commerce.[60]

61. Tobacco Curing Barns—Colonial America's First Specialty Structures

Tobacco curing barns were among the earliest specialized agricultural buildings in colonial America, designed specifically for drying and aging tobacco leaves. These barns used ventilation slats, wooden beams, and controlled airflow to ensure that tobacco cured properly, developing the signature flavors that made American-grown tobacco famous. Many historic tobacco barns from the 1700s and 1800s still stand today, offering a glimpse into the early days of tobacco farming.[61]

62. The Tradition of "Toasting" a Cigar Before Lighting

The ritual of "toasting" the foot of a cigar before lighting dates back centuries and remains an essential part of cigar etiquette. By slowly warming the cigar's foot over a flame without directly touching it, smokers ensure an even burn and prevent harsh, bitter flavors from developing. This technique, still practiced by cigar connoisseurs today, enhances the overall smoothness and complexity of the smoking experience.[62]

63. The Wrapper—The Biggest Contributor to a Cigar's Flavor

A cigar's wrapper leaf can contribute up to 70% of its overall flavor, making it the most influential part of a cigar's taste profile. The wrapper is the outermost layer, which burns first, releasing its natural oils and flavors. Whether it's a spicy Maduro, a creamy Connecticut Shade, or a bold Habano, the wrapper plays a key role in shaping a cigar's body, aroma, and complexity.[63]

64. The Invention of Cigar-Rolling Machines—A 19th Century Revolution

Before the late 1800s, all cigars were hand-rolled, but the invention of cigar-rolling machines dramatically changed the industry. These machines increased production speed, reduced costs, and made cigars more accessible to the mass market. However, purists argue that hand-rolled cigars remain superior, as machines cannot replicate the artistry of a skilled *torcedor* (cigar roller). Today, premium cigars are still hand-rolled, while machine-made cigars dominate the budget market.[64]

65. Cedar Spill Lighting—The Traditional Way to Fire Up

Long before butane lighters became the norm, cigar aficionados used thin, curled strips of Spanish cedar—known as cedar spills—to light their cigars. These spills provided a clean, aromatic flame that didn't alter the cigar's flavor like sulfur matches or lighter fluid might. Today, some premium lounges and old-school smokers still prefer the ritual of spill lighting, appreciating both the aesthetic and the respect it shows for the cigar's natural character. It's a nod to tradition that turns lighting up into a ceremony.[65]

66. Cuban Cigar Testing—A Professional Smoker's Job

Before some premium Cuban cigars are released to the public, they are tested by professional smokers, known as "catadores," who ensure perfect construction, burn, and flavor balance. These expert tasters assess everything from draw resistance to aroma, making sure only the finest cigars reach consumers. This rigorous quality control process is one of the reasons Cuban cigars maintain their reputation for excellence.[66]

67. Cigar Bloom (Plume)—A Sign of Quality Aging

When cigars are properly aged, they may develop a white, powdery substance known as "bloom" or "plume." This is caused by the natural oils in the tobacco rising to the surface, indicating that the cigar is aging well. Unlike mold, which appears as fuzzy green or blue patches, plume is harmless and can be gently brushed off. Many cigar aficionados consider plume a mark of a well-aged, high-quality cigar.[67]

68. The "Razor-Sharp Burn Line"—A Sign of a Well-Made Cigar

A well-constructed cigar should burn evenly, producing what's known as a "razor-sharp burn line." This clean, symmetrical burn is a hallmark of expert rolling and properly aged tobacco, ensuring a consistent smoking experience. If a cigar burns unevenly or "canoes" (burns more on one side), it may indicate poor rolling, improper humidity, or user error.[68]

69. Retrohaling—Unlocking Hidden Cigar Flavors

Retrohaling is a technique where smokers exhale cigar smoke through the nose, engaging the olfactory senses for a more complex flavor experience. Because the nose can detect thousands of aromas, retrohaling enhances the ability to pick up subtle notes like spice, wood, and leather that may go unnoticed with regular smoking. This method is commonly used by cigar aficionados and reviewers to fully appreciate a cigar's depth.[69]

70. Bill Clinton's White House Cigar Celebration—Breaking the No-Smoking Rule

After the 1995 rescue of U.S. pilot Scott O'Grady in Bosnia, President Bill Clinton lit a Romeo y Julieta cigar in the White House—reportedly defying a no-smoking rule set by First Lady Hillary Clinton. The brand, famously favored by Winston Churchill, symbolized victory and leadership. Whether Cuban or Dominican, the cigar became part of presidential cigar lore, showing that even world leaders make exceptions for a good smoke.[70]

71. Fidel Castro's Poisoned Cigar Assassination Plot

During the early 1960s, the Central Intelligence Agency (CIA) devised numerous schemes to eliminate Cuban leader Fidel Castro, capitalizing on his love for cigars. One such plan involved providing Castro with cigars laced with botulinum toxin, a potent poison. The intention was that upon smoking, the toxin would cause his immediate death.

This assassination attempt was part of a broader covert operation known as Operation Mongoose, aimed at destabilizing Castro's regime. The CIA collaborated with various individuals, including members of organized crime, to infiltrate Castro's inner circle and administer the poisoned cigars. However, this plot, like many others, was never successfully executed.

The poisoned cigar scheme is one of the numerous attempts documented in the 2006 British documentary "638 Ways to Kill Castro," which explores the extensive efforts to assassinate the Cuban leader.

Despite these relentless efforts, Fidel Castro remained in power for decades, often remarking on his survival amidst countless assassination plots.[71]

72. Catholic Missionaries and the Global Spread of Tobacco Cultivation

In the 16th and 17th centuries, Catholic missionaries, particularly the Jesuits, played a significant role in the dissemination of tobacco cultivation beyond the Americas. Recognizing tobacco's economic potential, the Jesuits established extensive tobacco plantations in Central and South America. They not only cultivated tobacco but also facilitated its spread by distributing tobacco seeds to various regions, thereby promoting its cultivation globally.

This widespread distribution led to tobacco becoming a lucrative commodity worldwide. The Columbian exchange further introduced tobacco to Europe, where it rapidly gained popularity and became an integral part of various cultures.

Regarding the claim about the Pope's stance on transplanting native plants, there is no historical evidence to suggest that any Pope opposed the relocation of plants like tobacco from their native regions to other parts of the world during that era.[72]

73. Winston Churchill's Cigars Had Their Own Oxygen Mask

Winston Churchill's love for cigars was so legendary that during World War II, a special oxygen mask was designed just for him—allowing him to smoke cigars while flying at high altitudes in unpressurized aircraft. This custom mask ensured that Churchill could enjoy his cigars even on dangerous wartime missions, proving that for him, cigars were just as essential as military strategy![73]

74. The FBI Used a Cigar Lounge to Bug a Mafia Boss

In 2011, the FBI placed a secret recording device inside a cigar lounge chair belonging to New York Mafia boss Joseph "Big Joe" Massino. The device captured him discussing crimes over cigars, providing key evidence that led to his conviction. This marked the first time a sitting Mafia boss became a government informant, all thanks to a well-placed cigar lounge bug![74]

75. The First Cigar Smoker Was Imprisoned for Witchcraft

Rodrigo de Jerez, a member of Columbus's first voyage, was likely the first European to smoke tobacco. When he returned to Spain in the 1490s and publicly exhaled smoke, his neighbors were terrified. Unfamiliar with the practice, they believed he was possessed—and the Spanish Inquisition allegedly imprisoned him for witchcraft.

Ironically, while Jerez sat in prison, tobacco use spread rapidly through Europe. By the time of his release, smoking had become a fashionable habit among the elite—a dramatic twist in the strange tale of tobacco's European debut.[75]

76. The Cigar Boom of the 1990s

A surge in cigar popularity during the 1990s, fueled by celebrity endorsements, luxury lifestyle branding, and economic optimism, led to a global cigar renaissance. Sales skyrocketed, new boutique brands emerged, and cigar lounges became cultural hotspots.[76]

77. The "Cigar of the Year" Effect

Being named *Cigar Aficionado's* "Cigar of the Year" can cause a brand's sales to double or triple overnight, often resulting in limited availability and secondary market price spikes.[77]

78. Tobacco Beetles—A Collector's Nightmare

Cigar beetles (*Lasioderma serricorne*) can destroy entire collections by boring holes through wrappers and filler. They hatch in temperatures above 72°F, which is why humidor temperature control is critical.[78]

79. The Difference Between Long-Filler and Short-Filler Cigars

Long-filler cigars use whole tobacco leaves, offering a smoother, more complex smoke. Short-filler cigars contain chopped pieces—often from leftover trimmings—making them less expensive but less refined.[79]

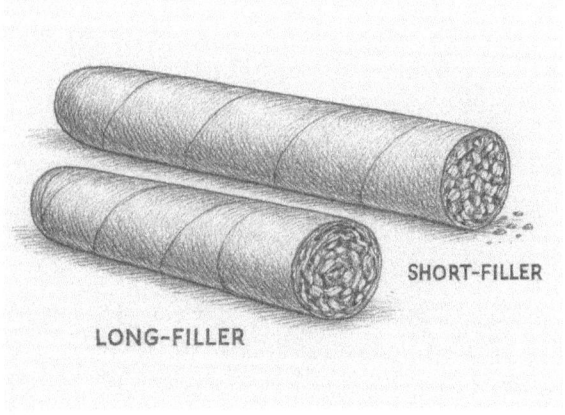

SHORT-FILLER

LONG-FILLER

80. The Role of Volado, Seco, and Ligero in a Blend

These are the three main types of filler leaves in a cigar. Volado provides combustion, Seco adds aroma and complexity, and Ligero delivers strength and boldness—together creating balance.[80]

81. Cigar Tasting Wheels—Mapping Flavor Notes

Like wine and whiskey, cigars have their own tasting wheels to help smokers identify flavors like cedar, leather, espresso, pepper, or cream. Developed by aficionados and sommeliers, these tools sharpen the sensory experience and enhance appreciation for complexity.[81]

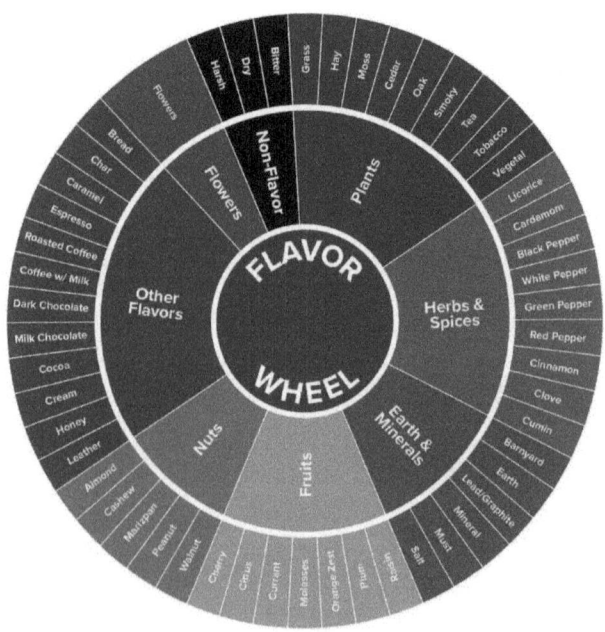

82. Cigar Box Art—A Forgotten Americana Collectible

Early cigar boxes featured ornate, colorful lithographs and embossed designs that became collectible pieces of American folk art. Some rare boxes fetch thousands at auction today.[82]

83. The Smoker's Cut vs. the Guillotine Cut

A "smoker's cut" is a diagonal slice that opens more surface area and can intensify flavor. While straight guillotine cuts are most common, V-cuts and punch cuts offer different draw profiles.[83]

84. The Influence of Soil—Cigar Terroir

Just like with wine, the flavor, aroma, and strength of tobacco are profoundly shaped by the soil in which it's grown—a concept known as terroir. Volcanic soils in Nicaragua yield bold, peppery notes due to high mineral content and porous drainage. In contrast, the red clay and limestone-rich soils of Cuba's famed Vuelta Abajo region contribute to cigars with exceptional balance, sweetness, and complexity. Even within the same country, subtle differences in elevation, rainfall, and soil composition can dramatically alter a tobacco's character. This is why discerning blenders often speak of tobacco like vintners speak of grapes.[84]

85. The "Fresh Roll" Cigars of Little Havana

In Miami's Little Havana, visitors can buy cigars rolled the same day—often just minutes before purchase. Known as "fresh rolls," these cigars are prized for their immediacy, vibrant aroma, and connection to Cuban tradition. Skilled artisans, many trained in Cuba or descended from Cuban torcedores, roll them by hand in full view of customers. The experience is as much about witnessing the craft as it is about enjoying the product. For many, smoking a fresh roll is a way to savor heritage, community, and authenticity—all in a single draw.[85]

86. Cigar Sommelier—A Real Job Title

Cigar sommeliers—also called tobacco sommeliers—are now found in luxury hotels, lounges, and fine dining establishments. These experts help guests pair cigars with spirits, coffee, or cuisine, curate humidor selections, and offer guidance on cutting, lighting, and tasting. Many undergo formal certification, with programs in the U.S., Europe, and the Dominican Republic. Blending hospitality with connoisseurship, the cigar sommelier elevates smoking into a personalized and refined experience.[86]

87. Rolling Without a Mold—The *Entubado* Technique

The traditional Cuban entubado method involves rolling each filler leaf into a tube before bunching them together and applying the wrapper. This labor-intensive process improves airflow, burn consistency, and flavor complexity. Unlike simpler methods, entubado requires more skill and time, which is why it's reserved for high-end, hand-rolled cigars. Though molds are often used in modern factories, many elite rollers still favor entubado for its superior draw and craftsmanship.[87]

88. The "Cold Draw" Ritual

Before lighting, aficionados often perform a "cold draw" to test airflow and sample the cigar's unlit flavor profile. By gently puffing on the cigar, smokers can detect earthy, sweet, woody, or grassy notes—often giving a preview of what's to come. It's also a practical step: a tight or plugged draw can reveal potential construction issues before the cigar is lit. For many enthusiasts, this brief moment enhances the anticipation and deepens appreciation for the craft behind each cigar.[88]

89. The Art of Cigar Aging—Cedar's Secret Role

Premium cigars are often aged in cedar-lined rooms, where the wood's natural oils gradually influence the cigar's aroma and flavor. Spanish cedar, in particular, is prized for its unique properties—it helps regulate humidity, wards off tobacco beetles, and imparts a subtle, woody fragrance that enhances the aging process. Over time, cigars stored in cedar-rich environments develop smoother, more refined characteristics. Whether in factory aging vaults or personal humidors, Spanish cedar remains the gold standard for traditional and effective cigar aging.[89]

90. The Double Claro (Candela) Wrapper—A Green Revival

Candela wrappers, once wildly popular in the U.S. during the 1950s and 1960s, are picked early and flash-cured using a rapid heat process that locks in their distinctive green hue. Known for their grassy, herbal notes and mild flavor, they were later dismissed as old-fashioned. But in recent years, they've seen a quiet revival among retro-smoking enthusiasts and boutique cigar makers aiming to reintroduce nostalgic styles with modern craftsmanship.[90]

91. Celebrity-Owned Cigar Brands

Actors like Arnold Schwarzenegger and Andy García, and musicians like DJ Khaled, Post Malone, and Yandel, have all partnered with or invested in boutique cigar brands. Some, like García, work closely on blending and branding, while others lend their image and lifestyle to high-end collaborations. These ventures not only reflect the celebrity's personal passion for cigars but also help introduce premium cigars to new and diverse audiences—blurring the lines between luxury branding, pop culture, and artisanal tobacco.[91]

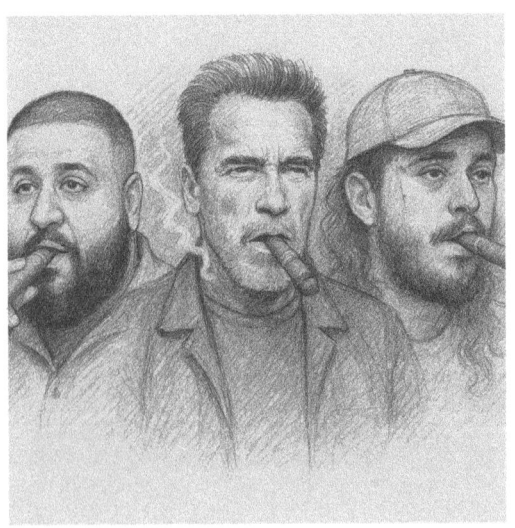

92. The Secret Language of Cigar Bands

Cigar bands do more than decorate—they communicate. Colors, emblems, and typography are used to signal strength, origin, lineage, or exclusivity. A red band might evoke intensity or bold flavor, while gold implies prestige or premium status. Shields, lions, or crowns often reference heritage or national identity, particularly in Cuban and Dominican labels. Typography styles, such as script or block letters, also subtly cue whether a cigar leans traditional or modern. For collectors and aficionados alike, cigar bands serve as miniature branding statements packed with meaning.[92]

93. Women in the Modern Cigar Industry

While women have long played essential roles in cigar rolling, their presence today extends across branding, blending, manufacturing, and executive leadership. Figures like Cynthia Fuente (Arturo Fuente) and Nirka Reyes (De Los Reyes Cigars) are helping reshape the industry from within—bringing innovation, refined palate sensibilities, and global market insight. Many female leaders are also pushing for storytelling rooted in heritage and craftsmanship, while attracting a more diverse generation of smokers. Their contributions are redefining what cigar leadership looks like in the 21st century.[93]

94. The Cigar That Survived the Titanic

While many items sank with the Titanic in 1912, a few unsmoked cigars in passenger luggage were later recovered by salvage divers. Though badly water-damaged, these relics became prized collectibles—testaments to the luxurious tastes of the ship's first-class passengers.[94]

95. The First Cigar Vending Machine Was Coin-Operated in 1883

Inventor Thomas Adams introduced the first commercial vending machine in U.S. train stations—selling single cigars for a penny. It marked the beginning of automated tobacco retail.[95]

96. Cigar Ash in Paint? Artists Say Yes

Some painters in the 19th century added cigar ash to their oil paints to create unique texture effects, claiming it enhanced matte finishes. Though more eccentric than standard, the technique found niche popularity.[96]

97. Cigar-Toting Action Figures? G.I. Joe Once Had One

In the 1980s, a limited-edition G.I. Joe "General Hawk" prototype was designed holding a cigar. It was never mass-produced due to marketing restrictions—but leaked prototypes remain rare collector's items.[97]

98. The Cigar Ring Gauge Tool Was Invented by a Watchmaker

The cigar ring gauge tool—a device used to measure a cigar's diameter—was originally adapted from a sizing tool used by watchmakers and jewelers. Known for their precision work, watchmakers used similar ring-sizing devices to calibrate fine parts. Early cigar manufacturers borrowed this concept to ensure consistency in cigar dimensions—an overlap between luxury crafts, where precision and presentation are essential to the final product.[98]

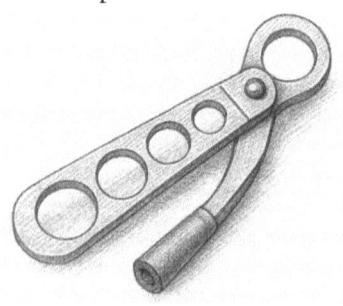

99. The Only MLB No-Hitter Celebrated with a Cigar… on the Field

After pitching a no-hitter for the Pittsburgh Pirates on June 12, 1970, Dock Ellis was famously seen lighting a cigar in the dugout—a rare sight in Major League Baseball. The act, though never officially fined, triggered mild backlash from league officials and the press, who viewed it as unsportsmanlike. Despite the media frenzy, Ellis' flair for provocation became part of his legend. The moment stands out in MLB history as one of the most unconventional no-hitter celebrations ever recorded.[99]

100. The Cigar-Shaped UFO—A Real Term in Ufology

In UFO sightings from the 1940s onward, many witnesses described unidentified flying objects as "cigar-shaped." The term stuck in popular alien lore and is still used by enthusiasts and researchers today.[100]

101. The "Cigar Store Indian" Was Actually a Marketing Gimmick

The carved wooden Native American figure outside tobacco shops in the 1800s served as a visual cue for the illiterate, symbolizing the link between Indigenous cultures and tobacco. Though often stylized inaccurately, it became a lasting—and controversial—icon of American advertising.[101]

List of Facts by Category

Part I: Ancient Smoke & Early Origins

Fact #1. Where Does the Word "Cigar" Come From?
Fact #2. The Oldest Known Image of a Cigar Smoker
Fact #3. Seville: The Birthplace of the Modern Cigar
Fact #4. The First U.S. Cigar Factory
Fact #5. Tobacco Farming in the American Colonies
Fact #44. The 600-Year-Old Cigar—An Ancient Find
Fact #48. Tobacco in Native American Peace & Diplomacy
Fact #50. Tobacco as a Sacred Offering in Native American Rituals
Fact #51. Early Tobacco Pipes—Artistic & Spiritual Masterpieces
Fact #60. The First North American Tobacco Plantation—Jamestown, 1612
Fact #61. Tobacco Curing Barns—Colonial America's First Specialty Structures
Fact #72. Catholic Missionaries and the Global Spread of Tobacco Cultivation
Fact #75. The First Cigar Smoker Was Imprisoned for Witchcraft

Part II: Politics, War & Power

Fact #6. The Cuban Cigar Ban That Changed Everything
Fact #7. JFK's Secret Stash of Cuban Cigars
Fact #9. Ulysses S. Grant and His 10,000 Cigar Gift
Fact #12. Fidel Castro and the Rise of Cohiba
Fact #13. The Origin of the Word "Stogie"

Fact #14. Civil War Soldiers Smoked & Traded Cigars on the Battlefield

Fact #15. The Lost Cigar Dispatch of 1862—Fact or Fiction?

Fact #18. Napoleon's Surprising Cigar Preference

Fact #21. Cigars in World War II Rations

Fact #23. Fidel Castro's Diplomatic Cigar Gifts

Fact #25. Cigars as a Political Power Symbol

Fact #29. Bill Clinton, Cigars & a Political Scandal

Fact #70. Bill Clinton's White House Cigar Celebration—Breaking the No-Smoking Rule

Fact #71. Fidel Castro's Poisoned Cigar Assassination Plot

Fact #73. Winston Churchill's Cigars Had Their Own Oxygen Mask

Fact #74. The FBI Used a Cigar Lounge to Bug a Mafia Boss

Part III: Icons & Aficionados

Fact #8. Mark Twain's Love Affair with Cigars

Fact #10. Freud's Cigar Obsession—And His Most Famous Quote

Fact #11. Winston Churchill—A Cigar Icon

Fact #19. Mark Twain's Love for Cheap Cigars—And His Famous Prank

Fact #26. Cigars in Hollywood—A Symbol of Wealth & Power

Fact #27. George Burns' 100-Year Cigar Habit

Fact #47. Writers & Their Cigar-Fueled Creativity

Part IV: Culture, Craft & Innovation

Fact #16. Tampa—The Cigar Capital of the U.S.

Fact #17. America's Cigar Boom—8 Billion Smokes a Year

Fact #22. The Cuban Tradition of Women Cigar Rollers

Fact #30. Cuban Cigars—100% Handmade, No Machines Allowed

Fact #31. Ligero—The Powerhouse of a Cigar

Fact #32. The Year-Long Journey of a Premium Cigar

Fact #33. Cigars Aged for Decades—The Arturo Fuente "Añejo" Legacy

Fact #34. The 70/70 Rule—How to Keep Your Cigars Fresh

Fact #36. Cigars Infused with Rum & Whiskey—A Flavorful Twist

Fact #39. Gurkha Cigars—The Brand Behind the World's Most Expensive Cigars

Fact #40. The Barber Pole Cigar—A Twisted Work of Art

Fact #Fact #49. The First Flavored Cigars—A 1900s Innovation

Fact #55. Hand-Painted Cigar Bands—A Lost Art

Fact #57. Coffee-Infused Cigars—A Bold New Flavor Trend

Fact #58. Tobacco Giants & Their Private Farms

Fact #59. The Evolution of Tobacco Aging—Pressure-Aging Experiments

Fact #64. The Invention of Cigar-Rolling Machines—A 19th Century Revolution

Fact #65. Cedar Spill Lighting—The Traditional Way to Fire Up

Fact #66. Cuban Cigar Testing—A Professional Smoker's Job

Fact #67. Cigar Bloom (Plume)—A Sign of Quality Aging

Fact #68. The "Razor-Sharp Burn Line"—A Sign of a Well-Made Cigar

Fact #86. Cigar Sommelier—A Real Job Title

Fact #87. Rolling Without a Mold—The Entubado Technique

Fact #89. The Art of Cigar Aging—Cedar's Secret Role

Fact #90. The Double Claro (Candela) Wrapper—A Green Revival

Part V: Myths, Legends & Oddities

Fact #20. The 11-Hour Cigar Smoking Session—Fact or Fiction?

Fact #37. Cigar-Smoking Geckos—Fact or Fiction?

Fact #38. The Longest Cigar Ash—A Fragile World Record?

Fact #41. The 12-Cigar Smoking World Record—Fact or Fiction?

Fact #42. "The Egg"—A Cigar Like No Other

Fact #56. The First International Cigar Competition—A Havana Mystery

Fact #96. Cigar Ash in Paint? Artists Say Yes

Fact #97. Cigar-Toting Action Figures? G.I. Joe Once Had One

Fact #100. The Cigar-Shaped UFO—A Real Term in Ufology

Part VI: Gender, Identity & Modern Trends

Fact #28. Madonna & the Cigar Industry's Gender Shift

Fact #91. Celebrity-Owned Cigar Brands

Fact #93. Women in the Modern Cigar Industry

Part VII: Ritual, Taste & Etiquette

Fact #62. The Tradition of "Toasting" a Cigar Before Lighting
Fact #69. Retrohaling—Unlocking Hidden Cigar Flavors
Fact #76. The Cigar Boom of the 1990s
Fact #77. The "Cigar of the Year" Effect
Fact #78. Tobacco Beetles—A Collector's Nightmare
Fact #79. The Difference Between Long-Filler and Short-Filler Cigars
Fact #80. The Role of Volado, Seco, and Ligero in a Blend
Fact #81. Cigar Tasting Wheels—Mapping Flavor Notes
Fact #83. The Smoker's Cut vs. the Guillotine Cut
Fact #88. The "Cold Draw" Ritual

Part VIII: Science, Farming & Terroir

Fact #63. The Wrapper—The Biggest Contributor to a Cigar's Flavor
Fact #84. The Influence of Soil—Cigar Terroir
Fact #85. The "Fresh Roll" Cigars of Little Havana

Part IX: Symbols, Fashion & Folklore

Fact #43. Smoking Jackets—Fashion Born from the Cigar Ritual
Fact #24. Cigar Box Tax Stamps—Tiny Artifacts of Tobacco History
Fact #45. Cigars—A Tradition of Celebration and Success
Fact #52. The Return of Cigar Bars—Old-School Luxury Makes a Comeback
Fact #53. High-Tech Air Filtration in Modern Cigar Lounges

Fact #82. Cigar Box Art—A Forgotten Americana Collectible

Fact #92. The Secret Language of Cigar Bands

Fact #98. The Cigar Ring Gauge Tool Was Invented by a Watchmaker

Fact #101. The "Cigar Store Indian" Was Actually a Marketing Gimmick

Part X: Law, Crime & the Underworld

Fact #46. Al Capone & the Crime Boss Cigar Symbol

Fact #94. The Cigar That Survived the Titanic

Fact #95. The First Cigar Vending Machine Was Coin-Operated in 1883

Fact #99. The Only MLB No-Hitter Celebrated with a Cigar… on the Field

Part XI: Markets, Celebrities & Global Influence

Fact #35. The World's Largest Cigar—A 295-Foot Masterpiece

Fact #54. Cigars & Poker—A Gambler's Good Luck Charm?

About the Author

J.R. Johnson is a certified cigar sommelier, spirits expert, and devoted history buff with a passion for the rituals and stories that linger in smoke. A collector of rare cigars and vintage narratives, he brings wit and depth to the cultural crossroads of tobacco, tradition, and taste. *Cigar Curious* is his most playful take on a lifelong obsession.

Also from The American Cigar Press

- *Smoke & Oak: The Shared Legacy of Bourbon and Cigars – An American Story of Craft, Culture & the Science of a Perfect Pairing* by Sebastian Saviano
  A richly illustrated journey through two of America's most iconic crafts, *Smoke & Oak* explores the intertwined histories, cultural significance, and sensory science behind bourbon and cigars. Includes a full-color pairing wheel and expert insights for enthusiasts and newcomers alike.

- *America's Cigar Story: The History, Politics, and Legacy of Cigars from 1762 to the Modern Era* by Sebastian Saviano
  A landmark cultural history tracing the rise, fall, and reinvention of the American cigar industry—from colonial trade and Civil War generals to political symbolism and modern craft revival.

Endnotes

[1] William Bright, *Native American Placenames of the United States* (University of Oklahoma Press, 2004).
Note: Usage of "seegar" found in 19th-century American newspapers and dialect-heavy literature (e.g., Twain, Huckleberry Finn).

[2] Karl Taube, *The Major Gods of Ancient Yucatan* (Studies in Pre-Columbian Art & Archaeology, 1992); and Johannes Wilbert, ed., *Tobacco and Shamanism in South America* (New Haven: Yale University Press, 1987).

[3] José Manuel Rodríguez Gordillo, *Historia de la Real Fábrica de Tabacos de Sevilla: sede actual de la Universidad de Sevilla* (Seville: Universidad de Sevilla, 2005), 59.

[4] Ana Cuenca, "Discover the Legacy of Primer Fábrica 1810: A Tribute to Cigar History," Cuenca Cigars, March 20, 2025.

[5] Ben Green and Michael D. Hartley, "Cigar Tobacco Production in Pennsylvania (PA)," *CORESTA Reports*, 2023

[6] Sebastian Saviano, *America's Cigar Story: The History, Politics, and Legacy of Cigars from 1762 to the Modern Era* (The American Cigar Press, 2025), 144–47.

[7] Saviano, *America's Cigar Story*, 148.

[8] Richard Carleton Hacker, "Samuel Clemens and His Cigars," *Cigar Aficionado*, November/December 1994

[9] J. Mark Powell, "The Gift That Killed General Grant," *Holy Cow! History*, March 17, 2021

[10] "Freud and His Cigars," *Freud Museum London*, April 22, 2020.
Note: The famous line "Sometimes a cigar is just a cigar" is apocryphal—never documented in Freud's works.

[11] J. Bennett Alexander, "Winston Churchill's Favorite Cigars," *Holt's Cigar Company*, May 8, 2018

[12] Gordon Mott, "50 Years of Cohiba," *Cigar Aficionado*, March/April 2016.

[13] "Stogie: Cigar of the Conestoga Wagoneer," *Uncharted Lancaster*, September 6, 2023.

[14] Tim Talbott, "Civil War Soldiers and Tobacco Use," *Random Thoughts on History*, November 9, 2020.

[15] "Special Orders No. 191," *National Park Service*.
Note: While widely reported in military lore and commemorated in historical markers, some historians question whether the cigars were truly part of the original discovery or added in retellings to dramatize the event.

[16] "Cigar Box Labels," *Museum of Florida History*.

[17] Sebastian Saviano, *America's Cigar Story: The History, Politics, and Legacy of Cigars from 1762 to the Modern Era* (The American Cigar Press, 2025), 188–91.

[18] Shannon Selin, "10 Interesting Facts About Napoleon Bonaparte," *Shannon Selin* (blog), October 2014.
Note: While Napoleon's use of snuff is well documented, there is no reliable evidence confirming a preference for Spanish cigars over Cuban ones.

[19] Alejandro Benes, "Samuel Clemens and His Cigars," *Cigar Aficionado*, Winter 1995;
Ted Anthony, "Close, But No Cigar Band," *Medium*, April 5, 2023

[20] "New Records, Upsets and Suspensions at the 2024 Cigar Smoking World Championships So Far," *Friends of Habanos*, July 4, 2024.
Note: No credible documentation exists; the story appears in anecdotal accounts and cigar folklore but lacks verifiable sources.

[21] "History of Tobacco in Military Rations," Flight Attendant Medical Research Institute (FAMRI).
Note: Historically accurate in some periods, especially during WWI and WWII, though not standard across all units or eras.

[22] Mottola, Gregory. "Master Cigar Roller Maria Sierra, 70, Dies." *Cigar Aficionado*, January 23, 2019.
Note: Maria Sierra is widely credited as one of the first formally recognized female cigar rollers in post-revolution Cuba, though others may have preceded her informally.

[23] Gordon Mott, "50 Years of Cohiba," *Cigar Aficionado*, March/April 2016.

[24] "Tobacco Tax Paid and Export Revenue Stamp Proofs," Smithsonian National Postal Museum, 1868, Object No. 2011.2005.703.

[25] Sebastian Saviano, *America's Cigar Story: The History, Politics, and Legacy of Cigars from 1762 to the Modern Era* (The American Cigar Press, 2023).

[26] Tamburino, Tyler. "The Art of the Cigar in Film." *Cigar Public*, January 9, 2025.

[27] Marx, Arthur. "The Ultimate Cigar Aficionado." *Cigar Aficionado*, Winter 1994/1995.

[28] Holt's Cigar Company. "Famous Women Who Smoked Cigars." *Holt's Cigar Company*.

[29] Starr, Kenneth W. *The Starr Report: The Findings of Independent Counsel Kenneth W. Starr on President Clinton and the Lewinsky Affair.* Washington, D.C.: U.S. Government Printing Office, 1998.

[30] Habanos S.A. *Unique Since 1492*. Havana: Habanos S.A., 2021.

[31] Holt's Cigar Company. "Ligero Cigars & Tobacco." *Holt's Clubhouse*, 2023.

[32] Davidoff of Geneva. "Davidoff's Creation – From Seed to Cigar." *Davidoff Geneva USA*. 2025.

[33] Marcus Daniel Tobacconist. "Very Rare Davidoff Millennium Cigars (Box of 20) - Vintage 2000 - Aged 24 Years." *Marcus Daniel Tobacconist*. 2025.

[34] NewAir. "What is the Best Temperature for a Cigar Humidor?" *NewAir*, 2018.

[35] Marsh, Sarah. "Long Life, Very Long Cigar: Cuban Dedicates a Monster Smoke to Fidel Castro." *Reuters*, August 13, 2016.

[36] Arturo Fuente. "Añejo." *Arturo Fuente*. 2025;
Drew Estate. "Brands." *Drew Estate*. 2025.

[37] No primary source—commonly repeated industry folklore with no scientific basis.

[38] No official documentation; claims originate from informal community contests and anecdotal reports.

[39] Heredia, Mariana. "What is the Most Expensive Cigar in the World?" *Cigar Country*, 2021;
Gurkha Cigars. "Gurkha Royal Courtesan." *Gurkha Cigar Group*, 2023.

[40] Cigar Aficionado. "What is a Barber Pole Cigar?" *Cigar Aficionado*, August 2019.

[41] CigarWorld.com forums; no verified Guinness record exists as of 2025.

[42] Cigar Aficionado. "Strange Cigars," *Cigar Aficionado* 2010.

[43] G. Bruce Boyer, *Elegance: A Guide to Quality in Menswear*, W.W. Norton, 1985.

[44] Joseph C. Winter, *Tobacco Use by Native North Americans: Sacred Smoke and Silent Killer* (University of Oklahoma Press, 2000).

[45] Richard Carleton Hacker, *The Ultimate Cigar Book*, Autumngold Publishing, 2022 (4th ed.).

[46] John Kobler, *Capone: The Life and World of Al Capone* (Da Capo Press, 2003).

[47] A.E. Hotchner, *Papa Hemingway: A Personal Memoir* (New York: Random House, 1966);
Rudyard Kipling, "The Betrothed," in *Departmental Ditties and Other Verses* (London: Macmillan & Co., 1886).

[48] Joseph Epes Brown, *The Sacred Pipe: Black Elk's Account of the Seven Rites of the Oglala Sioux* (Norman: University of Oklahoma Press, 1953);
Peter Jordan, "Tobacco Use in Native North America: An Overview," *Journal of Ethnopharmacology* 19, no. 3 (1987): 273–289.
Note: Styles vary widely by region and era, and pipes often held ceremonial as well as social significance.

[49] Drew Estate, "The ACID Cigar Revolution," Drew Estate Official Website;
Charles Sutliff, *The History of Aromatic Tobaccos in American Blending* (Tobacco Industry Archives, 1982).

[50] Porterfield, Amanda. *American Religious Traditions: The Sacred and the Secular in the History of Religion in America.* Lanham, MD: Rowman & Littlefield, 2005.

[51] National Museum of the American Indian. *Native American Pipes: Artistry and Meaning.* Smithsonian Institution, 2020.

[52] Cigar Aficionado. "Back in Vogue: Cigar Lounges Are Hot Again," *Cigar Aficionado*, April 2021.

[53] "Ventilation Design for Cigar Lounges," ASHRAE Journal, March 2020.

[54] "Smoke and Strategy: Cigars at the Card Table," *Card Player Magazine*, Issue 47, 2021.

[55] Holts Cigar Company. "Habanos Cigar Festival." *Holt's Cigar Company.*
Note: While widely circulated in cigar lore, there is limited historical documentation confirming the details of this 1935

Havana event. It may reflect industry legend rather than a formally recorded competition.

[56] Sebastian Saviano, *America's Cigar Story: The History, Politics, and Legacy of Cigars from 1762 to the Modern Era* (The American Cigar Press, 2025).

[57] Sebastian Saviano, *America's Cigar Story: The History, Politics, and Legacy of Cigars from 1762 to the Modern Era* (The American Cigar Press, 2025).

[58] Sebastian Saviano, *Smoke & Oak: The Shared Legacy of Bourbon and Cigars* (The American Cigar Press, 2025).
Note: It discusses brand-specific cultivation practices by Arturo Fuente, Davidoff, and Oliva.

[59] Sebastian Saviano, *America's Cigar Story: The History, Politics, and Legacy of Cigars from 1762 to the Modern Era* (The American Cigar Press, 2025).
Note: Supporting insights on experimental fermentation, advanced aging techniques, and boutique innovation in tobacco production can be found throughout the book, particularly in sections discussing controlled humidity environments, temperature-regulated aging, and the reimagining of cigar craftsmanship as a blend of science and artistry.

[60] "Tobacco in Colonial Virginia," *Encyclopedia Virginia*, Virginia Humanities.

[61] Lanier, Gabrielle M., and Bernard L. Herman. *Everyday Architecture of the Mid-Atlantic: Looking at Buildings and Landscapes.* Johns Hopkins University Press, 1997.

[62] Min Ron Nee. *An Illustrated Encyclopedia of Post-Revolution Havana Cigars* (2003).

[63] Encyclopedia of Cigars, by Sam Weller (2014).

[64] Reynolds, John L. *Tobacco Culture: The Mentality of the Great Tidewater Planters on the Eve of Revolution* (Princeton University Press, 1988).

⁶⁵ Cigar Aficionado. "The Art of Lighting a Cigar." *Cigar Aficionado*, various issues, 1994–2012.

⁶⁶ Gjelten, Tom. *Bacardi and the Long Fight for Cuba: The Biography of a Cause*. New York: Viking, 2008.

⁶⁷ Cigar Aficionado. "What Is Cigar Plume?" *Cigar Aficionado*, May 2006.

⁶⁸ Cigar Aficionado. "How to Light a Cigar." *Cigar Aficionado*, April 2005.

⁶⁹ Cigar Aficionado. "How to Retrohale Like a Pro." *Cigar Aficionado*, June 2013.

⁷⁰ Cigar Aficionado. "Clinton Lights Up After Rescue." *Cigar Aficionado*, August 1995.

⁷¹ Prados, John. *Safe for Democracy: The Secret Wars of the CIA*. Chicago: Ivan R. Dee, 2006.
Note: While the poisoned cigar plot is widely reported and referenced in multiple sources, including documentaries and declassified CIA materials, no verifiable evidence confirms the cigars were ever physically produced or delivered.

⁷² Gately, Iain. *Tobacco: A Cultural History of How an Exotic Plant Seduced Civilization*. New York: Grove Press, 2001.
Note: The involvement of Jesuit missionaries in tobacco cultivation is well documented, but no formal Vatican decree or papal opposition to transplanting plants has been recorded during this period.

⁷³ Soames, Mary. *Clementine Churchill: The Biography of a Marriage*. London: Doubleday, 2002.

⁷⁴ Rashbaum, William K. "A Don, a Tape and a Deal: How the F.B.I. Caught a Mafia Boss." *The New York Times*, June 23, 2011.

⁷⁵ Gately, Iain. *Tobacco: A Cultural History of How an Exotic Plant Seduced Civilization*. New York: Grove Press, 2001.

Note: The account of Rodrigo de Jerez being imprisoned by the Inquisition is a long-standing historical anecdote. While widely repeated, contemporary documentation confirming this exact cause for imprisonment remains elusive.

[76] Cigar Aficionado. "The Cigar Boom." *Cigar Aficionado*, Winter 1997.

[77] Halfwheel. "The Cigar of the Year Effect: Demand, Scarcity, and Speculation." *Halfwheel Reports*, January 2020.

[78] Cigar Aficionado. "Beetle Mania: What to Know." *Cigar Aficionado*, July 2006.

[79] Cigar Aficionado. "The Basics of Cigar Construction." *Cigar Aficionado*, March 2009.

[80] Cigar Aficionado. "Understanding Filler Tobacco." *Cigar Aficionado*, July 2012.

[81] Cigar Journal. "Flavor Wheels and Palate Training." *Cigar Journal*, Fall 2017.

[82] White, Jay. *The Art of the Cigar Label: Lithography and Advertising in the Gilded Age*. Cincinnati: Graphic Arts Press, 1999.

[83] Cigar Aficionado. "What's the Best Way to Cut a Cigar?" *Cigar Aficionado*, January 2010.

[84] Cigar Aficionado. "The Soil Makes the Smoke." *Cigar Aficionado*, October 2007.

[85] Cigar Aficionado. "Rolling in the Streets of Little Havana." *Cigar Aficionado*, March 2004.

[86] Tobacconist University. *Certified Cigar Sommelier Tobacconist (CCST) Program Curriculum*. Princeton, NJ: Tobacconist University Press, 2019.

[87] Tobacconist University. *Cigar Construction & Rolling Styles Manual*. Princeton, NJ: Tobacconist University Press, 2017.

[88] Cigar Aficionado. "The Cold Draw: First Impressions Matter." *Cigar Aficionado*, February 2014.

[89] Cigar Aficionado. "Inside the Aging Room: How Great Cigars Rest." *Cigar Aficionado*, March 2011.

[90] Richard Carleton Hacker, *The Ultimate Cigar Book*, 4th ed. (New York: Skyhorse Publishing, 2015), 84–86.

[91] Cigar Aficionado. "Andy García: A Life with Cigars." *Cigar Aficionado*, June 2005;
Cigar Aficionado. "DJ Khaled Launches 'Another One' Cigar with El Septimo." *Cigar Aficionado*, October 2022;
Cigar Snob. "Post Malone Collaborates on Shady Moose Cigars." *Cigar Snob*, July 2023.

[92] Cigar Aficionado. "Decoding the Cigar Band." *Cigar Aficionado*, July 2012.

[93] Cigar Journal. "The Rise of Women in the Cigar Industry." *Cigar Journal*, Autumn 2022.

[94] Cigar Aficionado. "Wreckage and Relics: Cigars on the Titanic." *Cigar Aficionado*, April 2012.
Note: Salvage reports confirm that cigars were recovered from the Titanic wreck, though most were unsmokable and preserved only for their historical value.

[95] Hacker, Richard Carleton. *The Ultimate Cigar Book*. 4th ed. New York: Skyhorse Publishing, 2015.

[96] Not a mainstream technique, but documented in niche art histories and memoirs of experimental painters of the late 1800s.

[97] "Prototype G.I. Joe Figures: Controversial Concepts." *YoJoe.com Archives*, last modified 2023.
Note: While never released to market, the prototype is documented in collector circles and toy forums, and images have surfaced, though official production was halted due to marketing concerns.

[98] Hacker, Richard Carleton. *The Ultimate Cigar Book*. 4th ed. New York: Skyhorse Publishing, 2015.

[99] Sports Illustrated. "Dock Ellis: High Heat." *Sports Illustrated Vault*, June 2010.

[100] Adamski, George. *Flying Saucers Have Landed*. London: Werner Laurie, 1953.

[101] Huber, Leonard V. "The Cigar Store Indian." *Louisiana History: The Journal of the Louisiana Historical Association* 9, no. 3 (1968): 197–206.

www.ingramcontent.com/pod-product-compliance
Lightning Source LLC
Chambersburg PA
CBHW060343010426
42229CB00021B/255